Life-Changing Prayers

Building Kingdom Consciousness

Dr. Doral R. Pulley

Dedication

I dedicate this book to Marques Clark and Harvey Pearlman.

Marques, one of my spiritual sons, held a Global Healing Summit on the grounds of Today's Church Tampa Bay in St. Petersburg, Florida. He had a vision to bring like-minded people together to make a difference on the planet. He invited me along with many other Spiritual Leaders and teachers to share their consciousness and their practices with others.

During my time of sharing, I was guided to share the Nine-Fold Baptism (found on pages 62 – 64). The energy that the prayer emanated was amazing. The prayer participants became one and it set the tone for the entire day. Several people remarked about how blessed they were by the prayer. One of the spiritual healers, Harvey Pearlman, invited me to lunch.

While at lunch, Harvey, requested a copy of the prayer and asked if it was copywritten. I had not thought to do so with the prayer. I was inspired write it down. As I was typing the prayer, I heard the whisper of the Holy Spirit saying, "compile a book of life-changing prayers." My first response was I'm too busy with the Kingdom Study Bible, other projects, and general responsibilities. I heard the voice a little louder and I said, "Yes."

Once I said, "YES!" I found over a hundred prayers that I had written over the years for myself and others. All of the prayers in this volume were carefully chosen, just for you.

Acknowledgments

I AM grateful for all those who supported me in this project: Bishop A. Bernard Hector, Deacon Renet Denard Cole, Minister Gina Folk, Overseer Samuel W. Hairston IV, Rev. Sheri James, Rev. Bernette L. Jones, Dr. Davina Jones, Colette M. Jones, Mother Linda Johnson, Rev. Sheree Thompson, Brittney R. Robinson, Courtney R. Pulley, D. Reginald Pulley II, David Richard Onuche, the Church of the Everlasting Kingdom, Today's Church Tampa Bay, the Father's Summit, and my Daily Download Family.

Introduction

We have often been told, "Prayer changes things." More importantly, prayer changes you and when you are changed, you are empowered to change the things in your life. Sometimes people want prayer to change other people, but they themselves do not want to change. Your life is full of systems: marriage, partnership, family, friendships, spiritual communities, businesses, educational institutions, neighborhoods, etc. Since you are part of these systems, when you change, the system changes.

Your family is a system, and, when you change through prayer, your family system changes. Your friendships are systems, and when you change through prayer, your friendship system changes. Your business or job is a system, and when you change through prayer, your career system changes. Your school is a system, and when you change through prayer, the educational system changes. Your neighborhood is a system, and when you change through prayer, the community system changes. Your local assembly is a system, and when you change through prayer, the religious system changes. The local government is a system, and when you change through prayer, the city changes. The state government is a system, and when you change through prayer, the state that you live in changes. The federal government is a system, and when you change through prayer, your country changes. This consciousness of positive change continues with all continents, cultures, planets, throughout the entire universe.

Prayer is a two-way communication between you and God. Through prayer, communication with God, you are empowered to change. The prayers in this book have been life-changing for me. These prayers have been developed to move individuals and communities from one state of awareness to another. Through this awareness, people have been able to do something different. They have been empowered to live the lives that they desire and deserve. I believe that they are worth sharing with others.

TABLE OF CONTENTS

Prayer Book V: Holiday & Special Occasion Life-changing Prayers 67

Prayer Book I:

Daily Life-Changing Prayers

> *"Blessed be the Lord, the God of our salvation, who daily loads us with benefits."* Psalm 69:18 KSB

INTRODUCTION

The prayers in this chapter are very diverse. They cover a gamut of needs and desires. They can be prayed daily, weekly, monthly, annually, or as needed until you feel complete and total peace. They can be prayed individually, with a prayer partner, or with a small or large group. Use them are you are guided by the Holy Spirit.

Most of the prayers were written through pure inspiration from the Holy Spirit through me. Some of them were influenced by other spiritual teachers, artists, and writers. When this is the case, the name of the influencer is noted to give honor where honor is due (Romans 13:7). Each of these life-changing prayers begin with a scripture from the Kingdom Study Bible that set the tone for the experience. The scriptures are ending truths. When you pray, read, or think a scripture, you join the collective consciousness of all those who have ever used the scripture in any way. This multiplies the energy of the prayer and makes for an easy flow of fruition.

How these prayers end is unique to the prayer itself. Some of them end with "in the name and through the power and in the consciousness of Christ Jesus." Ending prayers with "*in the name and through the power and in the consciousness of Christ Jesus.*" In *the name* means in the nature or character of Christ Jesus. Although other people were named Jesus, your prayer is about the image that comes in mind when you say the name. *"Through the power"* is a reminder that there is Only One Power and One Presence in the Universe. The same power that Jesus Christ used is you the same power you can use now and get the same results. *"In the consciousness of Christ Jesus"* means that you are aware of Jesus' development from Jesus (human) to Jesus Christ (both human and divine) to Christ Jesus (divinity first, humanity second). In this awareness, you can focus on your divinity and what God can do through you (Philippians 4:13).

Others end with "it is so, so it is, and so I/we let it be." These endings speak of your understanding of who you are, whose you are, and your divine right to decree and declare what you desire (Job 22:28, Romans 4:17). There is no specific reason as to why a prayer ends a particular way. It is simply how I was guided when I wrote the prayer. No ending is more powerful or effective than another. Regardless of how the prayers conclude, they are life changing.

"I lack nothing.
I have learned in whatever state
that I AM in to be content."
Philippians 4:11 KSB

THE CONTENTMENT PRAYER

I release the idea of comparing myself to others.

I AM a unique unrepeatable expression of the Divine.

I AM content with who I AM.

I let go of competing with others.

I have a particular path.

I have a unique journey.

I AM content with where I AM.

Contention has no power over me.

My life flows with the ease and breeze of Spirit.

I AM content with what I have.

I AM content right here and right now.

It is so, so it is, and so I let it be.

> "Be strong and very courageous
> for the Lord, your God,
> will be with you wherever you go."
> Joshua 1:9 KSB

THE COURAGEOUS PRAYER

I have the courage to be who God created me to be.

I have the courage to say what God commands me to say.

I have the courage to do what God calls me to do.

I have the courage to go where God commissions me to go.

I have the courage to have everything God promised me.

It is so, so it is, and so I let it be.

> "For we are laborers together with God.
> We are God's field.
> We are God's building."
> I Corinthians 3:9 KSB

THE CREATIVE PRAYER

Life is creatable.

Life is not fixed.

I AM co-creating with God the life that I desire.

I AM co-creating with God the life that I deserve.

It is so, so it is, and so I let it be.

"To this end,
I contend with all the energy
that Christ so powerfully works in me."
Colossians 1:29

THE ENERGY PRAYER*

I have endless energy to do what is mine to do.

I pay attention to who and what energizes me.

I pay attention to who and what drains me.

I protect my energy.

I AM in control of my energy and what I do with it.

I channel my energy in a positive direction.

I realize that all my emotions are energy in motion.

I channel my energy to be productive, not destructive.

Through my positive energy, I create climates.

Through my positive energy, I set atmospheres.

Through my positive energy, I lift up the energy on the earth.

Through my positive energy, I lift up the vibration in the universe.

Influenced by Charles Roth

"It is God working in you
both to will and to do
of God's good pleasure."
Philippians 2:13 KSB

THE EXPANSION PRAYER

I AM the Everlasting Energy,

Expressing through the Events of my life,

Calling for Soulful Experiences,

That I may be Educated,

My life Enriched,

And the consciousness of the Universe Expanded

Through my sharing.

It is so, so it is, and so I let it be.

"The light of the body are the eyes.
When your eyes have a singular focus,
then your whole body is full of light."
Matthew 5:22 KSB

THE FOCUS PRAYER

Today, I focus on the person that I desire to become and the goals that I desire to achieve.

I AM not double-minded for double-minded people are unstable in all their ways (James 1:8).

I have the Mind of Christ (I Corinthians 2:16).

I AM not double-tongued (I Timothy 3:8).

I allow the Holy Spirit to guide my words (Matthew 10:20).

I do not live a double life (Matthew 23:28).

My life is hid with Christ in God (Colossians 3:3).

I make to focus on living a holistically healthy, balanced, and well-rounded life.

It is so, so it is, and so I let it be.

> "I desire to know and experience Jesus
> in the power of his resurrection,
> in the fellowship of his sufferings,
> and in his death."
> Philippians 3:10

THE FIFTH DIMENSION PRAYER

I AM grateful that I know you in the fifth dimension.

You are Savior. You have redeemed my life from destruction.

You have awakened me to my divinity.

I AM savior. I help people wake up to the truth of their being.

You are Christ.

You were anointed with the Holy Spirit and power.

You went about doing good and healing all diseases.

When people see me, they see Christ.

I decrease and allow the Christ in me and as me to increase.

You are the Lord of lords.

I AM lord.

I do not lord over others.

I lord over myself and control my thoughts, words, and actions.

You are the King of kings.

I AM king (queen, royalty).

I reign in my domain and exercise dominion in my assigned areas.

You are the God of gods.

I AM god.

I show up wherever you send me manifesting my divinity.

It is so, so it is, and so I let it be.

Amen. Amen.

8

"For you will show me the path of life.
In your presence is the fullness of joy
and at your right hand there are pleasures
that last forever."
Psalm 16:11 KSB

THE FULFILLMENT PRAYER

In the presence of God, there is only fullness.

There is no emptiness in God's presence.

There is no lack in God's presence.

There are no voids in God's presence.

There are no vacancies in God's presence.

In the presence of God, I AM filled full.

In the presence of God, I AM fulfilled.

It is so, so it is, and so I let it be.

> "For the Lord is good.
> God's mercy is everlasting.
> God's truth endures to all generations."
> Psalm 100:5 KSB

THE GOODNESS PRAYER

There is no separation between me and God.

There is no separation between me and my good.

God withholds no good thing from me (Psalms 84:11).

My good is coming to me NOW from the supernatural realm to the natural realm.

My good is coming to me NOW from the heavenly realm to the earthly realm.

My good is coming to me NOW from the spiritual realm to the physical realm.

My good is coming to me NOW from the invisible to the visible.

My good is coming to me NOW from the intangible to the tangible.

I believe it and I receive it NOW by faith. (Hebrews 11:1).

It is so, so it is, and so I let it be.

"Give as you have purposed in your heart,
not out of fear or obligation
because God loves a cheerful giver."
2 Corinthians 9:7 KSB

THE GIVING PRAYER

Giving is receiving.

I freely give and I freely receive.

I give my time and I receive more time.

I give my talents and I receive more opportunities to share my talents.

I give my treasure and I receive more money.

I give cheerfully and abundance is drawn to me like a magnet.

I give liberally and I receive liberally with no strings attached.

"Beloved, I wish above all things
that you prosper and be in health
even as your soul prospers."
2 John 1:3 KSB

THE HEALING PRAYER

My spirit is wholeness.

My soul is healing.

My body is manifesting that health.

It is so, so it is, and so I let it be.

"Do not be deceived.
God is not mocked.
Whatever people sow,
they will reap."
Galatians 6:7 KSB

THE HARVEST PRAYER

My life is my harvest.

The Universe is fertile soil.

My thoughts plant the seeds of my life.

I think positive words.

My words water the seeds that I have planted.

I speak positive words.

My actions fertilize the seeds that I have planted.

I do positive actions.

The Universe provides sunlight to seeds that I have planted.

I weed out erroneous ideas.

I weed out limiting beliefs.

I weed out faulty perceptions.

I allow the process of seed, time, and harvest.

Any harvest that I do not like, I can change.

I can change the thoughts that I think and plant new thoughts.

I can change the words that I speak and water my life with new words.

I can change the actions that I do and fertilize my life with new actions.

It is so, so it is, and so I let it be.

"This book of the law will always be in your mouth.
You will meditate on it day and night.
You will pay close attention to it
and do all the things that are written in it.
Then you will be prosperous
and successful in whatever you do."
Joshua 1:8 KSB

THE LIMITLESS PRAYER

My good is not limited to a particular person or type of people.

I AM successful with all people who cross my path.

My good is not limited to a particular day, season, or time.

Every day is my day.

Every season is my season.

Every time is my time.

My good is not limited to a particular place or space.

I AM prosperous and successful in all places and spaces.

My good is not limited to particular thing that I do.

Whatever I do is prosperous and successful.

It is so, so it is, and so I let it be.

"That all of them may be one, Father,
just as you are in me, and I AM in you.
I desire for them to also be one with us
so that the world may believe
that you have sent me."
John 17:21 KSB

THE ONENESS PRAYER

I AM one with God.

I AM one with Good.

I AM one with all spiritual beings,

I AM one with all manifestations of human beings.

I AM one with all forms of life.

Angels and Animals.

Vegetation and all nature.

I AM one with the One.

There is Only One.

It is so, so it is, and so we let it be.

Amen. Amen.

"As an even exchange,
I open my mouth to you
as a parent speaks to their children,
open your hearts wide to receive."
2 Corinthians 6:11 KSB

THE OPENNESS PRAYER

I open my heart and my mind to receive love.

I open my heart and my mind to receive joy.

I open my heart and my mind to receive peace.

I open my heart and my mind to receive prosperity.

I open my heart and my mind to receive forgiveness.

I open my heart and my mind to receive grace and mercy.

I open my heart and my mind to receive optimal health.

I open my heart and my mind to receive harmonious relationships.

I open my heart and my mind to receive effective communication.

I open my heart and my mind to receive complete understanding.

I open my heart and my mind to receive positive interactions.

I open my heart and my mind to receive safety.

I open my heart and my mind to receive security.

I open my heart and my mind to receive support.

I open my heart and my mind to receive worldwide travel.

I open my heart and my mind to receive adventure and ecstasy (Genesis 22:14).

It is so, so it is, and so I let it be.

> "I know the thoughts that I think about you
> and the plans that I have for you,
> says the Lord, plans to give you hope,
> a future, and an expected end."
> Jeremiah 29:11 KSB

THE POSITIVE PRAYER*

I AM a positive person.

I serve a positive God.

I pray positive prayers.

Therefore, I get positive results.

It is so, so it is, and so I let it be.

Influenced by Hypatia Hasbrouck

"For in you is the fountain of life.
In your light, we see light."
Psalm 36:9 KSB

THE PROSPERITY PRAYER

Prosperity is a fountain that flows.

Prosperity is always flowing unless I block it.

I remove all blocks.

I allow my prosperity to flow.

I remove all barriers.

I allow my prosperity to flow.

I remove all boulders.

I allow my prosperity to flow.

My prosperity is flowing as optimal health.

My prosperity is flowing as harmonious relationships.

My prosperity is flowing as overflowing wealth.

I believe it and I receive it now.

It is so, so it is, and so I let it be.

"The earth, in all of its fullness,
belongs to the Lord,
everyone and everything are the Lord's."
Psalm 24:1 KSB

THE SOURCE PRAYER

God is my Source.

Everyone and everything else in my life is a resource.

I receive all of the resources, channels, and conduits

That God flows through to bless me.

It is so, so it is, and so I let it be.

Amen. Amen.

"Do not be conformed to this world
but be transformed by the renewing of your mind
so that you can prove what is the good,
acceptable, and perfect will of God."
Romans 12:2 KSB

THE TRANSFORMATIONAL PRAYER

I AM not a leopard. I can change my spots.

I AM not a zebra. I can change my stripes.

I AM spiritual being. I have the power to change.

I can grow. I can heal.

I can forgive. I can unfold.

I can become. I can change.

It is so, so it is, and so I let it be.

> "In him was life,
> and that life was the light
> of all humankind."
> John 1:4 KSB

THE UNIVERSAL LIFE PRAYER*

There is only one life and that is God's life.

God is living God's life through me.

God's life is flowing through me empowering me to fulfill God's purpose for my life.

God's life is manifesting through us as optimal health.

God's life is manifesting through me as harmonious relationships.

God's life is manifesting through me as overflowing wealth.

People who are about life are drawn to me.

People who are about life connect to me.

People who are about life partner with me.

It is so, so it is, and so I let it be.

Influenced by Eddie Watkins, Jr.

"When people purge themselves from these,
they will vessels of honor, sanctified,
fit for the Master's flow,
and prepared for every good work."
2 Timothy 2:21 KSB

THE VESSEL PRAYER

I release and I let go of being an instrument

That is picked up and put down.

I AM God's vessel.

God abides in me always and forever.

I AM a pure vessel.

God flows through me to bless others.

I keep my spirit free.

I keep my heart pure.

I keep my conscious clear.

It is so, so it is, and so I let it be.

Prayer Book II:

Life-Changing Prayers for Specific Manifestations

> *"And blessed is she who believed: for there will be a manifestation of all those things which the Lord told her through the angel."* Luke 1:45 KSB

INTRODUCTION

One of the ways to powerfully use the scriptures in your life is through finding scriptures that apply to an experience that you are having. You can find applicable scriptures through any search engine. I use Google or biblegateway.com. Once you find the appropriate scripture, you can speak it with power along with a denial and an affirmation to build your consciousness around the ideas of optimal health, harmonious relationships, and overflowing wealth. Denials disempower your fears, doubts, and worries so that you can speak your affirmation with power and authority.

The combination of quoting scripture together with denials and affirmations forms a Prayer Tool that helps you communicate what you desire to bring into manifestation. Think of a hammer. Quoting scripture is the handle, the universal truth. Denials are the claw pulling up old ideas and limiting beliefs that firmly planted and nailed into your consciousness. Affirmations are the head that securely fastens the good desires of your heart.

Several of the prayers for specific manifestations in this chapter have a scripture, a denial, and an affirmation. Some of them are affirmative prayers which clearly and concisely state the good desires of our hearts. No matter what the format, the prayers in this chapter will change your life. These prayers can also serve as a template for other prayer requests that may not be stated in this chapter. Feel free to modify them and make them your own so that you can bring into fruition the good desires of your heart.

BUSINESS

<u>Scripture</u> – "My God supplies all of my needs according to the riches and glory that are in Christ Jesus (Philippians 4:19)." KSB

<u>Denial</u> - My current employment does not limit my ability to be an excellent entrepreneur.

<u>Affirmation</u> – I ask and give thanks for the right and perfect business opportunities with a net profit of _____ or more. I receive this or something greater in the name and through the power and in the consciousness of Christ Jesus. It is so and so it is! Amen.

COMFORT

I wrap you and your family in the healing light of God's love for comfort and strength during this challenging time of transition. I pray that the transition of your loved one brings family and friends closer together as you support one another. Know that I AM God's manifested presence who is here for you and willing to serve in whatever capacity needed. It is so, so it is, and so I let it be. Amen. Amen.

COURT

I pray for the judge, lawyers, jurors, plaintiffs, defendants, and those involved in this case. I pray for the highest and best outcomes for all parties involved. It is so, so it is, and so we let it be. Amen. Amen.

EXAMPLE

Scripture – "Follow me as I AM also a follower of Christ (I Corinthians 11:1)!" KSB

Denial - I AM not a hypocrite, fake, or phony.

Affirmation - Following the footsteps of my Wayshower, Jesus Christ, I lead by example. I practice all of the principles that I pray, preach, and prophesy. I manifest my good first and then I inspire others to do the same. I demonstrate holistic growth and development, harmony in all my relationships and interactions, wealth, and success right here and right now. It is in the name and through the power and in the consciousness of Christ Jesus that it is so and so it is! Amen and Amen.

EMPLOYMENT

Scripture – "There is nothing better than to enjoy food, drink, and to find satisfaction in work. Then I realized that all these pleasures are from God's hands (Ecclesiastes 2:24)." KSB

Denial - I release all thoughts that suggest that I will not receive the highest and best job for me. I let go of any feelings that I do not deserve this ideal job.

Affirmation - I ask and give thanks for the right and perfect employment opportunity in my field with the right and perfect salary, benefits, schedule, and opportunities for advancement. I envision working in a team environment where I am completely accepted and where I support others in their progress for the greater good of the community that we are called to serve.

FIDELITY

Scripture – "Delight yourself also in the Lord and God will give you the desires of your heart (Psalm 37:4)." KSB

Denial - I release and let go of the limited idea that I have to cheat, flirt, fantasize, or watch pornography to be sexually satisfied.

Affirmation - Holy Spirit, thank you for helping me heal whatever needs to be healed in me soulfully and physically so that I can be the right and perfect romantic and sexual partner for my spouse as evidenced by mutually satisfying erotic pleasure and fulfilling sensual experiences, whenever we make love. It is so, so it is and so I let it be. Amen. Amen.

HEART ISSUES

We hold the consciousness of healing, health, and wholeness for those who have experienced heart attacks, those impacted by a person who has had a heart attack, and those at risk of heart attacks. It is in the name and through the power and in the consciousness of Christ Jesus that it is so, so it is, and so we let it be.

JEALOUSY

Scripture: "Love is strong as death; jealousy is cruel as the grave." Song of Songs 8:6 KSB

Denial: I release and let go of jealousy. I do not need to be jealous of anyone.

Affirmation: We are all one. We are all the same.

26

MINISTRY

We hold the consciousness for spiritual, numerical, financial, and physical growth of this ministry. We are true to our identity. We are living out our vision. We are fulfilling our mission. We are reaching our short-term and long-term goals. We are operating according to our core values. We are manifesting the meaning of our colors, logo, symbols, and slogans in everything that we do. We are attracting people of desire what we have to offer and who are willing to grow with us. It is so, so it is, and so we let it be.

PARTNER

I agree with you in prayer for the right and perfect partner who is a mirror reflection of God's love for you. I see you two having a balanced relationship where you have things in common with each other and are complementary to each other. I picture you two communicating well and compromising when necessary. I envision you two becoming one in your love for God, in your love for yourselves, and in your love for one another. I hold the vision of you two making each other's lives better, accomplishing goals in solidarity, and fulfilling destiny together. It is so, so it is, and so we let it be. Amen. Amen.

SURGERY

I pray for the doctors, nurses, technicians, and all those attending to your care. I see you having a successful surgery and a full and speedy recovery.

Prayer Book III:

Personal Life-Changing Prayers

"I sought the Lord, and God heard me, and delivered me from all my fears." Psalm 34:4

INTRODUCTION

One of the most powerful things you can do as a human being is to pray for yourself. One of the greatest accomplishments of this life is developing a consistent, open, and honest dialogue with your Creator, God. "The effectual fervent prayer of a righteous person avails much (James 5:16)." KSB

Your prayer life may begin with someone praying for you because you do not know how to pray. It may have started with an awareness of the truth that you can talk directly to God for yourself. The origin of your prayer life may begin with a spiritual awakening that there is a God in which to pray. Maybe you asked someone to pray for you because you were angry with God or disenchanted by those who represent God. Someone may have jumped started your prayer experience by sharing with you their testimony of the power of prayer. Regardless of how it starts, the goal is for you to learn to pray for yourself.

I began praying a child just walking and talking to God. Since I was an only child, when I felt alone or had no one to talk to, I talked to God. Often, I heard God talk back to me. Prayer became my go to when I was happy, sad, lonely, bored, angry, or having a challenge in my life.

In this chapter, I become vulnerable, and I share with you my personal prayer life. You will see one of the ways that I start my day and how I have overcome various character defects. This chapter is also about how I processed grief and healed myself of disease. The goal is to inspire you to develop life-changing prayers that help you overcome the challenges in your life.

> "I AM Alpha and Omega,
> the beginning and the ending,
> says the Lord,
> I AM, I was, and I will always be,
> the Almighty."
> Revelation 1:8

THE ALPHABET PRAYER

I AM an anointed apostle.

I AM a brilliant bishop.

I AM a compassionate counselor.

I AM a devoted dad

I AM an excellent establishmentarian.

I AM a faithful friend.

I AM a grateful grandfather.

I AM a holy husband.

I AM an ingenious innovator.

I AM a just judge.

I AM a keen king.

I AM a loving leader.

I AM a metaphysical minister.

I AM a natural navigator.

I AM an optimistic oasis.

I AM a powerful preacher.

I AM a quality quotient.

I AM a righteous ringleader.

I AM a successful son.

I AM a talented teacher.

I AM a unified universalist.

I AM a victorious visionary.

I AM a wonderful writer.

I AM a xeniaxenium.

I AM a yearning youth.

I AM a zealous Zion.

> "Then your light will break through like the dawn,
> and your healing will quickly appear.
> Then righteousness will go before you,
> and the glory of the Lord will be your rear guard."
> Isaiah 58:8 KSB

BACK CHALLENGES*

I AM not alone.

I AM loved.

I AM supported.

I AM not abandoned.

God has my back.

I have a team of people who support me.

I have a network that has my back.

It is so, so it is, and so I let it be.

Amen. Amen.

Influenced by Louise Hay

"Then Jesus declared, "I AM the bread of life.
Whoever comes to me will never be hungry,
and whoever believes in me will never be thirsty."
John 6:35 KSB

CONSCIOUS LIFE DESIGN PRAYER*

Spiritually

I AM lovingly living all the truth that I know.

Individually

I AM happy about my holistically healthy, balanced, and well-rounded life.

Relationally

I AM completely accepting of myself and others as I enjoy mutually fulfilling experiences wherever I AM, especially where I live.

Life Work

I AM filled with overflowing love and joy as I encourage and support others on their love journey and wholeness path.

Community

I AM inspired and exhilarated as I consciously led communities who discover and develop the Christ light in themselves and in others.

Inspired by Rev. Bernette L. Jones

"Praise the Lord, O my soul,
and do not forget
all of God's benefits.
God forgives all your sins
and heals all your diseases."
Psalm 103:2-3 KSB

DIABETES HEALING PRAYER*

Thank you, diabetes for serving your purpose in my life.

You have been my teacher for the past 8 years.

I have the lesson and blessing from you.

I have rediscovered the love, joy, peace, and sweetness within myself.

Therefore, I don't have to look for it in food, beverages, and other people.

Diabetes, I release and let go.

You can now return to the nothingness from which you came.

Inspired by Myrtle Filmore

HIGHER CONSCIOUSNESS

> *"The one who is slow to anger is better than the mighty and the person who engages in self-control is greater than people who take cities."* Proverbs 16:32 KSB
>
> *"The person who does not exhibit self-control is like a broken city that is without walls."* Proverbs 25:28 KSB

Holy Spirit, with your help, I will not function in my lower consciousness. I will operate in my higher consciousness, the Christ Mind, the I AM of being so that I can manifest my highest good with all people and in all situations.

"We have the Mind of Christ (I Corinthians 2:16)." KSB

I will not function in my lower consciousness of lasciviousness. I choose to operate in my higher consciousness, the Christ Mind, the I AM of being and I manifest temperance which is self-control.

"I will keep them in perfect peace whose mind is focused and stayed on me (Isaiah 26:3)." KSB

I will not function in my lower consciousness of poor stewardship of resources (time, talents and treasure) that God has given me. I choose to operate in my higher consciousness, the Christ Mind, the I AM of my being and I manifest good stewardship which expresses as prosperity, increase, abundance, overflow and more than enough in my life, in my world and in my affairs.

"Whatever is true, honest, just, pure, lovely, and positive producing a good report, think about that. Those thoughts will manifest praise to God and virtue for you (Philippians 4:8)." KSB

I will not function in my lower consciousness of running away from issues and relationships. I choose to operate in my higher consciousness, the I AM of my being, the Christ Mind and I manifest longevity in relationships.

"For I know the thoughts that I think toward you, says the Lord, thoughts of peace and not of evil to give you peace, a future, and a life of fulfilled expectations (Jeremiah 29:11)." KSB

I will not function in my lower consciousness of selfishness and control. I choose to operate in my higher consciousness, the I AM of my being, the Christ Mind and I manifest care, concern, and consideration for others.

"Let this mind be in you which was also in Christ Jesus who being in the image and likeness of God thought it not robbery to be equal with God (Philippians 2:5)." KSB

I will not function in my lower consciousness of hypocrisy and dualism. I choose to operate in my higher consciousness, the I AM of my being, the Christ Mind and I manifest authenticity and genuineness in all of my interactions.

"People are what they think in their hearts (Proverbs 23:7)." KSB

I will not function in my lower consciousness of lies and deceit. I choose to operate in my higher consciousness, the I AM of my being, the Christ Mind and I manifest truth and integrity.

"*And the peace of God which surpasses all human understanding will keep your heart and your mind through Christ Jesus* (Philippians 4:7)." KSB

I will not function in my lower consciousness of justifying my wrong. I choose to operate in my higher consciousness, the I AM of my being, the Christ Mind and I manifest openness and honesty.

It is in the name and through the power and in the consciousness of Christ Jesus, it is so and so it is.

> "Some plant, others water,
> but only God can give the increase
> and make it grow
> (I Corinthians 3:7)." KSB

THE INCREASE PRAYER

I AM a powerful people developer who lives a holistically healthy, balanced, and well-rounded life.

There is a multi-million-dollar life-changingWORD in my mind, in my mouth and in my hands.

It is changing millions of lives and impacting thousands of communities for the good.

It is bringing millions of dollars to me, to my family and all those who are connected to me.

God promised me the I.N.C.R.E.A.S.E. of the 5, the 50, the 500, the 5000 and the Miracle Buildings.

Regardless of circumstances and appearances, God is not a liar.

I believe and I receive it now.

It is so, so it is and so I let it be.

In the name and through the power and in the consciousness of the Christ Jesus it so and so it is. Amen. Amen.

LIFE LESSONS AND BLESSINGS

Pastor Elizabeth Thompson - *my spiritual father... When she made her transition, she was unhappy and unfulfilled. I am not unhappy, and I am not unfulfilled. I AM happy. I AM fulfilled.

"For I have given you an example, that you are to follow. When you know and do these things you will experience happiness beyond your imagination (John 13:15)." KSB

Renee's LaNita McCree - my mother...When she made her transition, she was poor. I AM not poor. I AM wealthy and prosperous.

"Wealth and riches are in my house and your righteousness endures forever (Psalms 112:3)." KSB

Alecia Renee Pulley – the mother of my twin daughters...When she made her transition, she was uncertain about her purpose and the next steps for her life. I am not uncertain about my purpose. I AM sure about who I AM and what I AM called to do (preaching, teaching, writing, developing people, and leading entities).

"You have not chosen me, but I have chosen you. I have ordained you to go and produce fruit. Your fruit will produce fruit and whatever you ask the Father in my name you will receive (John 15:16)." KSB

Charles T. Thompson, Sr. - my grandfather...When he made his transition, he had cancer. I will not allow anything to eat at me. I have no guilt, no shame, and no condemnation about anything that I have done or anywhere that I have been. I AM healthy. I AM whole.

"There is therefore now no condemnation to them who are in Christ Jesus. They do not live according to the pattern of this world. They live in the Spirit (Romans 8:1)." KSB

Asbury Reginald Pulley – my father...When he made his transition, he was addicted to alcohol. I AM not addicted to any other person, substance, or behavior. I AM free. I AM temperance.

"All things are lawful for me, but all things are not beneficial for me. I will not be controlled by any person, place, or thing (I Corinthians 16:12)." KSB

The Rev. Dr. Mary A. Tumpkin – my spiritual mother...When she made her transition, she was unbalanced. I AM not unbalanced. I live a holistically healthy, balanced, and well-rounded life.

"I wish above all things that you prosper and be in health even as your soul prospers (III John 1:2)." KSB

LaNita B. Brown – my grandmother... When she made her transition, she was alone and lonely. I AM not alone. I AM not lonely. I have love in my life. I enjoy loving, committed, lifetime relationships.

"Whoever finds a spouse finds a gift and has obtained the Lord's favor (Proverbs 18:22)." KSB

In the name and through the power and in the consciousness of Christ Jesus, it is so and so it is.

*Spiritual fathers have nothing to do with gender. It is about their role in your life.

Prayer Book IV:

Life-Changing Prayers for Groups

> *"Where two or three are gathered together in my name, there I AM in the midst of them."* Matthew 18:20

INTRODUCTION

When you pray with another person, you join forces with them and multiply spiritual energy in a particular direction. The scripture supports the power of multiple persons and declares that one can chase a thousand, but two can put ten thousand to flight (Deuteronomy 32:30).

Jesus taught that there is a great power on earth when two people come into agreement about one thing. He promised that if two people agree concerning anything that our God will do it for us (Matthew 18:19). God honors unity and harmony so much that when two people from different backgrounds with unique perspectives come together as one, God promises to give them what they desire.

Although the prayers in this chapter were designed for prayer groups or with a prayer partner, you can work with them individually and achieve a measure of success. The greatest value of these prayers is for you to learn not only to pray one-on-one, just you and God but to also learn how to pray with others.

THE DIVINITY PRAYER

Affirmation of the Kingdom Principle of Divine Nature

Divine Nature – I AM one with God. "I and my Father are one (John 10:30)." KSB

There is Only One Power and One Presence in the Universe active in my life, in my world and in my affairs. It is God, the Good, Omnipotence, Omnipresence and Omniscience. God is the everywhere evenly present, Spirit of Absolute Good.

I recognize the goodness of God in myself. I behold the Christ in everyone else. I see the goodness of God in everything because my heart is pure. Blessed is the pure in heart for they shall see God (Matthew 5:8).

There is no separation between me and God. I AM one with God. I AM one with all forms of life. I AM one with the One.

"Nothing can separate me from the love of God which is in Christ Jesus our Lord. Neither death, nor life, nor angels, nor demons, nor principalities, nor powers, nor things present, nor things to come, nor height, nor depth; nothing in all of creation can separate me from the Love of God which is in Christ Jesus (Romans 8:38-39)."

God's love is perfect. God's love is universal. God's love is everlasting. God's love is unconditional. There is nothing that I can do to make God love me any more than he already does. There is nothing that I can do to make God love me any less. God's love for me is unconditional. There has never been a time in my life and there will never be a time in my life where God does not love me.

God's love for me is everlasting. There is no person who does not deserve or experience God's love. God's love is universal.

I AM a partaker of God's divine nature. I have escaped the corruption that is in the world through lust. I have received exceeding great and precious promises. God has given me all things that pertain unto life and godliness through the knowledge of him who has called me to glory and virtue (II Peter 1:1-4).

The nature of God is love. Therefore, I love God with all my heart, with all my soul and with all my mind. I love myself as God loves me. I love my children. I love my family. I love my friends. I love everyone else in that order. It is just that simple (Matthew 24:34-40).

Just as a cup of water from the ocean is the same as the water in the ocean itself only differing in the size of the container that holds the water, I AM one with God (John 14:9).

Affirmation of the Kingdom Principle of Divine Purpose

Divine Purpose

There is a divine purpose for my life that must be fulfilled, and I cannot make my transition from this dimension of life to the next dimension of life until that purpose is fulfilled.

I understand that purpose to be _____

I understand that purpose to be _____

I understand that purpose to be _____

I understand that purpose to be _____

I understand that purpose to be _____

All things work together for my good because I love God, I have been called according to his purpose. Through every experience that I have on this earth, I AM being conformed into the image of Christ (Romans 8:28-29).

"And be not conformed to this world but be transformed by the renewing of your minds that you may prove what is that good, acceptable, and perfect will of God (Romans 12:2)." KSB

Even what people mean for evil, God means for my good because God is all there is. There is nothing else but God in different degrees, in different forms, and in different manifestation. God is the only show in town. There is nothing else playing out in my life, but God which is my good (Genesis 45:1-8, 50:20).

Affirmation of the Kingdom Principle of Divine Order

Divine Order

There is a Divine Order in the universe and everything that happens in my life is happening according to that Divine Order. Everything in my life is happening exactly the way that it is supposed to.

There are no accidents. There are no incidents. There are no coincidences. There are no mistakes. There are "no wouldas." There are "no shouldas." There are "no couldas." There are no "if onlys." When I recall the Principle of Divine Order, I have no regrets because I know the Truth that everything in my life is divinely orchestrated by God.

I AM a good person and the steps of a good person are ordered by the Lord (Psalms 37:23).

I AM a spiritual being and every part of me functions in divine order according to the purpose that God made it.

Because he that is joined to the Lord is one with him in spirit, I AM no longer single. My spirit is married to the Holy Spirit; therefore, my spirit is divine order.

My soul which includes my mind, my emotions, my intellect and my will, all function in divine order.

My body functions in divine order. Every system, organ, cell, membrane, and tissue functions in divine right order.

Everything in my house functions in divine right order.

My vehicles function in divine right order.

My local assembly functions in divine right order.

My ministries function in divine right order.

My businesses function in divine right order.

My staff functions in divine right order.

My _____ functions in divine right order.

My _____ functions in divine right order.

My _____ functions in divine right order.

My _____ functions in divine right order.

My _____ functions in divine right order.

Every organization to which I am attached to or a part of functions in divine right order.

Affirmation of the Kingdom Principle of Divine Timing

Divine Timing

Everything in my life is happening exactly when it is supposed to. I AM not ahead of God. I AM not behind God, but I AM perfectly in tune and in step with God's divine timing for my life.

"I humble myself under the mighty hand of God and God exalts me in due time (I Peter 5:6)." KSB

"Promotion does not come from the east, the west, nor the south. But God is the judge. God humbles one and exalts another (Psalms 75:6)." KSB

"The race is not given to the swift, nor the battle to the strong, nor bread to the wise, nor riches to people with great understanding, nor favor to those who have skill; but time and chance happen to them all (Ecclesiastes 9:11)." KSB

I AM like a tree planted by the rivers of water. I bring forth my fruit in my season (Psalms 1:3).

And when the fullness of time was come, God brought forth beloved offspring. I AM God's offspring and in the fullness of time God brings me forth (Galatians 4:4).

I have come to the Kingdom for such a time as this (Esther 4:14).

I have no need to hurry. I have no need to worry. I have no need to rush or to procrastinate because everything in my life is happening exactly when it is supposed to (Matthew 6:28-33).

Affirmation of the Kingdom Principle of Divine Placement

Divine Placement

I AM exactly where I AM supposed to be. I can't be where I AM not. I can only be where I AM. Therefore, I show up to this time, to this place, to this space fully present, open and ready to receive all of the lessons and all of the blessings that God has planted in this place for me.

I AM exactly where I AM supposed to be spiritually.

I AM exactly where I AM supposed to be mentally.

I AM exactly where I AM supposed to be emotionally.

I AM exactly where I AM supposed to be physically.

I AM exactly where I AM supposed to be geographically.

I AM exactly where I AM supposed to be financially.

I AM exactly where I AM supposed to be educationally.

I AM exactly where I AM supposed to be vocationally.

I AM exactly where I AM supposed to be relationally.

I AM exactly where I AM supposed to be socially.

I have learned in whatsoever state that I AM in; therewith, to be content (Philippians 4:11).

"Godliness with contentment is great gain (I Timothy 6:6)" KSB

Affirmation of the Kingdom Principle of Divine Provision

Divine Provision*

Everything that I need, I have. If I don't have it NOW, then I don't need it NOW. But when I need it, I will have it.

The Lord is my shepherd. I shall not want. I lack nothing. There is no lack or limitation in my life (Psalms 23).

I delight myself in the Lord and God gives me the desires of my heart (Psalms 37:4).

My God supplies all of my needs according to his riches and glory in Christ Jesus (Philippians 4:19).

Therefore, I receive abundance, increase, overflow and more than enough so that I can give to people out of my saucer but never out of my cup (Psalms 23:5).

I AM a conduit through which God channels resources to bless other people (Luke 6:38).

Jehovah Jireh is my provider; therefore, all of my needs are met in full and on time today (Matthew 6:32-33).

Money in my hands is elastic. It stretches. Money in my hands multiplies like yeast (Ecclesiastes10:19).

I AM the righteousness of God and wealth is transferred to me (Proverbs 13:22, II Corinthians 5:21).

God has given me power to get wealth and I use that power to manifest wealth in my life, in my world and in my affairs (Deuteronomy 8:17-18).

Wealth and riches are in my house today (Psalms 112:3).

I have a net worth of more than _____ today. I have more than _____ in the bank today and no debt today. I enter the next dimension of my life debt-free, wealthy, and prosperous.

I wrap myself in the violet light of self-love and forgiveness.

I wrap myself in the white light of oneness with others.

I wrap myself in the gold light of prosperity.

The blessings of God make me rich, and God adds no sorrow to it (Proverbs 10:22).

I AM willing and obedient, and I eat the good of the land (Isaiah 1:18).

Influenced by St. Germain

Affirmation of the Kingdom Principle of Divine Protection

Divine Protection

I AM divinely protected by God.

I honor the Lord. I reverence the Lord. I fear the Lord.

I respect the Lord; therefore, the angels of the Lord are encamped around me, my family, my friends, my_____(Psalms 34:7).

There is a hedge of protection around us and anything that gets through that hedge of protection and gets to us was meant to be for God's glory and for our good (Job 1:10).

God has not given me the spirit of fear but of love, of power and of a sound mind (II Timothy 1:7).

No weapon formed against me shall prosper and every tongue that rises up against me in judgment I shall condemn it because my righteousness is of thee says God for this is the heritage of the children of God (Isaiah 54:17).

The Lord is my helper; I will not fear what people can do unto me (Hebrews 13:6).

"The Lord is my light and my salvation. Whom shall, I fear? The Lord is the strength of my life of whom shall I be afraid (Psalms 27:1-2)?" KSB

If God be for me, who then can be against me (Romans 8:31)?

I acknowledge, I affirm, I accept, and I appreciate ministering angels as they do their work to help bring about everything that I have affirmed in this prayer today (Matthew 4:11, Hebrews 1:14).

In the name and through the power and in the consciousness of Christ Jesus, it is so and so it is.

Amen and Amen.

THE KINGDOM PRAYER

Today, I consciously and purposely choose to live my life according to Kingdom Principles and I manifest the Kingdom Promises of optimal health, harmonious relationships, and overflowing wealth.

And it is the Father's good pleasure to give me the Kingdom (Luke 12:32).

I seek first the Kingdom and God's righteousness and all things are being added to me right here and right now (Matthew 6:33).

The Kingdom of God is a system, a dimension, a form of government, a way of being, seeing, thinking, speaking, and behaving in which God is the center.

"The Kingdom of God is not meat, drink, anything physical, or temporal but it is righteousness, peace, and joy in the Holy Ghost (Romans 14:17)." KSB

The Kingdom of God is the king's-domain. It is the place where the King rules and reigns. Behold, the Kingdom of God is within me (Luke 17:21).

The Kingdom of God is manifested when God's will in heaven is being done on the earth.

Your Kingdom come; Your will be done on earth as it in heaven.

Your Kingdom is a Kingdom of **love**. There is no hatred, no envy, no jealousy, no strife, no malice, no bitterness and no unforgiveness in God's Kingdom.

Your Kingdom come; Your will be done on earth as it is in heaven.

Your Kingdom is a Kingdom of **joy**. There is no sorrow, no sadness, no discontentment, and no depression in God's Kingdom.

Your Kingdom come; Your will be done on earth as it is in heaven.

Your Kingdom is a Kingdom of **peace**. There is no conflict, no confusion, no chaos, no battles, and no war in God's Kingdom.

Your Kingdom come; Your will be done on earth as it is in heaven.

Your Kingdom is a Kingdom of **prosperity**. There is no poverty, no recession, no limitation and no lack in God's Kingdom.

Your Kingdom come; Your will be done on earth as it is in heaven.

Your Kingdom is a Kingdom of **healing, health, wellness, and wholeness**. There is no illness, no sickness, no pain, no disease, no discomfort, and no distress in God's Kingdom.

Your Kingdom come; Your will be done on earth as it is in heaven.

Your Kingdom is a Kingdom of **wisdom, knowledge and understanding**. There is no ignorance, no illiteracy, and no stupidity in God's Kingdom.

Your Kingdom come; your will be done on earth as it is in heaven.

Your Kingdom is a Kingdom of **liberty and freedom**. There is no bondage, no addiction, no imbalance and no slavery in God's Kingdom.

Your Kingdom come; your will be done on earth as it is in heaven.

Your Kingdom is a Kingdom of **unity and equality**. There is no discord, no division, no racism, no ageism, no sexism, no homophobia, no classism, no discrimination, no prejudice, no isms and schisms in God's Kingdom.

Your Kingdom come; your will be done on earth as it is in heaven.

Your Kingdom is a Kingdom of **righteousness and holiness**. There is no sin, no offence, no transgression, no trespass, no iniquity, and no abomination in God's Kingdom.

Your Kingdom come; your will be done on earth as it is in heaven.

Your Kingdom is a Kingdom of **light and truth**. There is no darkness, no deceit, no lies, no hypocrisy, and no dishonesty in God's Kingdom.

Thy Kingdom come; thy will be done on earth as it is in heaven.

It is in the name, through the power, and in the consciousness of Christ Jesus.

It is so, so it is, and so I let it be.

Amen and Amen.

MASTER MIND PRAYER*

God is the Master Mind with the Master Plan for our lives. The purpose of a Master Mind group is to get like-minded, positive, proactive people together who have the Mind of Christ and want support in their lives and want to support other people's lives using the power of prayer (I Corinthians 2:16).

"Where two or three are gathered together in my name there I am in the midst of them (Matthew 18:20)."

"If two of you shall agree on earth as touching anything that they shall ask, it shall be done for them of my Father which is in heaven (Matthew18:19)."

Song – *"We have come into this house to gather in your name to worship you, worship you (3 times).*

To worship Christ within, worship Christ, Christ within." Bruce Ballinger

1. WE SURRENDER

We admit that, of ourselves, we are powerless to solve our seeming problems, powerless to improve our lives. We need God's help.

"I AM the vine, you are the branches: he that abides in me, and I in him, the same brings forth much fruit: for without me you can do nothing. If you abide in me and my words abide in you, you shall ask what you will and it will be done unto you (John 15:5-7)."

Song – *"I will do a new thing in you (2 times. Whatever you ask for, whatever you pray for, it shall not be denied saith the Lord, saith the Lord (the Law)."* Sandra A. Tayborn

2. WE BELIEVE

We have come to believe that God, the Master Mind, the One Power, and the One Presence in the Universe, is greater than ourselves and is responding to us in a personal way changing our lives for the good.

"With people this is impossible but with God all things are possible (Matthew 19:26)."

Song – *"We have come this far by faith, leaning on the Lord (the Law), trusting in his holy Word, he never failed me yet. Oh, Oh, Oh, Oh, Oh, can't turn around, we've come this far by faith."* Rev. Milton Biggham

3. WE UNDERSTAND

We now realize that erroneous self-defeating thinking is the cause of our seeming problems, unhappiness, fears, and failures. We are ready to have our belief system completely altered so our lives can be transformed by the renewing of our minds (Romans 12:1-2).

"People are what they think in their hearts (Proverbs 23:7)." KSB

Song – *"Be still and know that I AM God (3 times). Trust in the Lord with all thine heart (3 times). Wait on the Lord and be of good courage (3 times)."* Stephen Curtis Chapman

4. WE DECIDE

We make a conscious decision to surrender our will and our lives to the Master Mind. We ask and are willing to be changed at depth so that God's Master Plan can be fulfilled in our lives.

"Nevertheless, not as I will but your will be done (Matthew 26:39)."

Song – "*I have decided to follow Jesus (3 times) no turning back (2 times).*" Leslie B. Tucker

5. WE FORGIVE

We forgive ourselves for all of our seeming mistakes and shortcomings. We also forgive and release all other persons who seem to have injured or harmed us in any way.

"When you stand praying, forgive (Mark 11:25)."

Song – "*Your grace and mercy brought me through. I am living this moment because of you. I want to thank you and praise you too. Your grace and mercy brought me through.*" Mississippi Mass Choir

6. WE ASK

We make known our specific requests to God, the Master Mind with the Master Plan. We ask God and give thanks (*Response to each request – it is so and so it is*):

Corporate Requests:

For the right and perfect _____.

For the right and perfect _____.

For the right and perfect _____.

For the right and perfect _____.

For the right and perfect _____.

For the success of _____.

For the success of _____.

For the success of _____,

For the success of _____.

For the success of _____.

Individual Requests (*Response to each request – it is so and so it is*):

"Verily, verily, I say unto you, whatsoever ye shall ask the Father in my name, he will give it you (John 16:23)."

Song – *"It's done. What I shall be, I already am. It's done. God has worked it out on my behalf. My eyes may not see it. By faith, I receive it. It will manifest. It's already done."* Anita Wilson

7. WE GIVE THANKS

We give thanks that the Master Mind is responding to our needs and we assume the same feelings that we would have if our requests were fulfilled right here and right now.

"In all things give thanks for this is the will of God in Christ Jesus concerning you (I Thessalonians 5:18)."

Thank you, God for guiding us and helping us.

Thank you, God that we have open, honest communication with ourselves and others.

Thank you, God that we always experience overflowing joy.

Thank you, God that we are always open and receptive to divine unlimited ideas.

Thank you, God that we always express divine love to guide our every thought and action in this process.

Song – *"Thank you, Lord (3 times) I just gotta thank you Lord. You been so good (3 times) I just gotta thank you Lord. You made a way (3 times) I gotta thank you Lord. You changed my life (3 times) I just gotta thank you Lord."* Andre Crouch

8. WE DEDICATE

We dedicate our lives now. We now have a covenant in which it is agreed that the Master Mind is supplying us with an abundance of all things necessary to live a successful, happy, healthy, and prosperous life.

My God supplies all my needs according to God's riches and glory that are in Christ Jesus (Philippians 4:19).

We dedicate ourselves to be of maximum service to God and those around us; to live in a manner that sets the highest example for others to follow; and remain responsive in God's guidance.

"As we have therefore opportunity, let us do good to all people, especially to those who are of the household of faith (Galatians 6:10)." KSB

We go forth with a spirit of enthusiasm, excitement, and expectancy.

The joy of the Lord is my strength (Nehemiah 8:10).

I AM at peace.

"I will keep them in perfect peace whose minds are focused and stayed on me (Isaiah 26:3)." KSB

In the name and through the power of Christ Jesus, it is so, so it is and so we let it be!

Song – *"If you abide in me and my words abide in you then you shall what you will, and it shall be given unto you."* Helen Baylor

*Influenced by Rev. Jack Boland

THE NINE-FOLD BAPTISM*

Opening Prayer

Focusing on your breath, take a deep conscious cleansing breath

God breathed into human nostrils the breath of life and we became living souls.

And breathe

As we breath we become more of the beloved offspring of God that we already are.

And breathe

The Psalmist David said let everything that has breath Praise the Lord, Praise ye the Lord.

And breathe

As we consciously breathe, we are giving God thanksgiving, praise, and worship.

And breathe

As we consciously breathe, we are being filled full and fulfilled in the Holy Spirit

And breathe

First-Fold Baptism

Placing your hands on your stomach and affirm

God in me.

And breathe

Second-Fold Baptism

Bringing your hands from the stomach, up to the face and out to the atmosphere and affirm

God flowing through me.

And breathe

Third-Fold Baptism

Placing your hands in front of your face and down to the stomach and affirm

God functioning as me.

And breathe

Four-Fold Baptism

Lifting your hands above your head and affirm

God above me taking me to higher realms of consciousness

And breathe

Five-Fold Baptism

Placing your hands as far down as you can and affirm

God beneath me grounding me in the truth

And breathe

Six-Fold Baptism

Stretching out your left hand to your side and affirm

God beside me to my left keeping me from distraction

And breathe

Seven-Fold Baptism

Stretching out your right hand to your side and affirm

God beside me to my right keeping me from discouragement

And breathe

Eight-Fold Baptism

Bending and placing your hands behind your back and affirm

God behind me clearing up the wreckage of my past

And breathe

Nine-Fold Baptism

Stretching your hands in front of you and affirm

God before me setting the tone for my future

And breathe

Closing Prayer

God is all there is.

There is nothing else but God.

In various degrees and in various forms, it is all God.

It is always God.

Therefore, we take a moment to reflect on the goodness of God in ourselves,

the goodness of God in everyone else,

the goodness of God in everything else,

and we are knowing the truth today that all is well.

Amen. Amen.

Influenced by St. Germain

THE WAYSHOWER PRAYER

I AM God's beloved offspring. I AM made in the image of God. I AM made in the likeness of God (Genesis 1:26-28).

Everything that Jesus Christ was, I AM.

I AM Savior.

I AM Christ.

I AM Lord.

I AM King (I AM royalty).

I AM god.

Everything that Jesus Christ said about himself, I can say about myself.

I AM the light of the world.

I AM the salt of the earth.

I AM a city set on a hill that cannot be hid.

I AM the living water.

I AM the bread of life.

I AM the way.

I AM the truth.

I AM the life.

I AM the door.

I AM the Good Shepherd.

I AM the true vine.

I AM the resurrection and the life.

Everything that Jesus Christ did, I can do and even greater works (John 14:12).

I can preach with power.

I can teach with authority.

I can heal the sick.

I can raise the dead.

I can cast out devils which are negative influences.

I can change the atmosphere.

I can empower the blind to see.

I can empower the deaf to hear.

I can empower the dumb to speak.

I can empower the lame to walk.

I can cleanse the lepers/those with seemingly incurable diseases.

I can forgive sins.

I can feed the multitudes naturally and spiritually.

I can turn water into wine.

I can walk on water.

I can speak to the elements of nature, and they obey my voice.

I can speak those things which be not as though they were until they are.

The truth is that I can do all things through Christ which strengthens me (Philippians 4:13).

Prayer Book V:

Holiday & Special Occasion Life-Changing Prayers

> *"Therefore, let us come boldly to the throne of grace, that we may receive mercy, and find grace to help in time of need."* Hebrews 4:16

INTRODUCTION

As a Spiritual Leader, it has been my role to lead prayer in various spiritual communities where I have served. I have also been invited to lead other spiritual leaders and faith communities in prayer for various occasions. I believe that every occasion is an occasion to pray.

This chapter will take you through the American calendar year with the various holy days and holidays that are commonly celebrated. It will also provide you with sample prayers for plethora of life experiences that can occur during the course of a year. There are scriptural passages at the end of each prayer for further study and reflection. Again, these are sample that can be prayed just as they are, or they can be adopted to fit the occasion.

A New Years' Day Prayer

Thank you, God, for a new year.

This new year is like every new day

An opportunity for us to be new.

A new me and a new you.

We embrace a new way of being.

Our energy and our aura reflect the Christ of our being.

We embrace a new way of seeing.

We look at things from the divine perspective.

We embrace a new way of thinking.

We have and operate in the Mind of Christ.

We embrace a new way of speaking.

We speak death to the old and life to new.

We embrace a new way of behaving.

We do things that are the highest and the best.

Thank you, God, for a new day,

A new year,

A new dawn.

It is so, so it is, and so we let it be.

Amen. Amen.

Read: Psalm 96

A PRAYER FOR THE REV. DR. MARTIN LUTHER KING, JR. HOLIDAY

As the Rev. Dr. Martin Luther King, Jr. embodied the consciousness of Jesus Christ,

Let us follow him as he followed Christ.

Let us see each man as our brother.

Let us see each woman as our sister.

Let us see each child as our child.

Let us see each person as our sibling because we all are God's beloved offspring.

Let us treat each person the way that we desire to be treated.

Let us feed the hungry.

Let us hydrate the thirsty.

Let us house the homeless.

Let us clothe the naked.

Let us visit those who are in mental, emotional, and physical prisons.

Let us visit those who are challenged with sickness, pain, disease, discomfort, and dysfunction in their bodies.

Let us be the answer to the question.

Let us be the solution to the seeming problem.

Let us be the resolution to the issues of our day.

It is so, so it is, and so we let it be.

Amen. Amen.

Read: Matthew 25:31-46

A VALENTINE'S DAY PRAYER

As we celebrate Valentine's Day,

Let us return to the center and essence of who we really are, Pure Love.

Place your hands on your stomach.

Take a deep conscious breath.

In this moment, feel the energy of love.

In this moment, know the truth that you are loved.

In this moment, know that all people are loveable.

This love does not begin and end with us.

Love begins and ends with God.

God is love.

God is universal love.

God is everlasting love.

God is unconditional love.

God is perfect love.

I love God.

I AM learning to love myself more and more every day.

I AM sharing this love with more and more people every day.

It is so, so it is, and so I let it be.

Read: I Corinthians 13

AN EASTER PRAYER FOR RESURRECTION

Following the example of Jesus Christ,

We rise from the temptations and tests that felt like crucifixion.

We rise from the graves of our trials and tribulations.

We rise from the headaches and pains that seemed to bury us.

We rise to be our best selves and to live our best lives.

We rise to honor ourselves without dishonoring others.

We rise to love, joy, and peace.

We rise to unity and equality.

We rise to an earth that works for everyone.

We know what we are rising from.

We know what we are rising to.

Therefore, we can always rise again.

Thank you, God, for the power and hope of resurrection.

It is so, so it is, and so we let it be.

Amen. Amen.

Read: I Corinthians 15:35-58

A MOTHERS' DAY PRAYER

Thank you, God, for all mothers.

Thank you, God, for those who mother us in so many ways.

We bless all mothers,

Mothers Past

Mother Present

Mothers to be

Stepmothers

Godmothers

Grandmothers

Den Mothers

Team Moms

House Mothers

Dorm Mothers

Surrogate Mothers

Spiritual Mothers

Church Mothers

And all those who nurture us both naturally and spiritually.

May we all grow in our ability to manifest, maintain, and multiply.

It is so, so it is, and so we let it be.

Amen. Amen.

Read: Ephesians 6:1-3

A MEMORIAL DAY PRAYER

As we remember the soldiers who gave their lives in service to our country,

As we pray for the families that have been impacted by the transition of their loved ones,

Let us all discover a purpose that is bigger than this life.

It is so, so it is, and so we let it be.

Amen. Amen.

Read: Matthew 16:24-28

A FATHER'S DAY PRAYER

Thank you, God, for all fathers.

Thank you, God, for those who father us in so many ways.

We bless all fathers,

Past Fathers,

Present Fathers,

Fathers to be,

Stepfathers,

Godfathers,

Grandfathers,

Team Dads,

Surrogate Fathers,

Spiritual Fathers,

Coaches,

Mentors,

Church Patriarchs,

And all those who provide for us and protect us both naturally and spiritually.

May we all grow in our ability to have fortitude, to forgive, and to plan for our futures.

It is so, so it is, and so we let it be.

Amen. Amen.

Read: I Corinthians 4:8-16

A JUNETEENTH PRAYER

We align with the consciousness of freedom that manifested on this day many decades ago.

We know the truth today.

We are free from any human limitations and inhuman acts.

We know the truth today.

We are free from any physical burdens.

We know the truth today.

We are free from any mental bondage.

We know the truth today.

We are free from any emotional baggage.

We know the truth today.

We are free to live, love, laugh, and be the light that we are.

It is so, so it is, and so we let it be.

Read: John 8:31-41

A PRIDE PRAYER

We celebrate the strength and the courage to be open and honest about who we love.

And we realize that we are all on a love journey and a wholeness path.

We pray that those who do not accept us learn to tolerate us.

We pray that those who tolerate us learn to accept us.

We pray that those who accept us learn to celebrate us

So that each person will be celebrated for who they are

And where they are in their lives.

As much as love lives within you, live in peace with all people.

It is so, so it is, and so we let it be.

Amen. Amen.

Read: Matthew 5:1-12

AN INDEPENDENCE DAY PRAYER

As we celebrate our independence as a country,

Let us be free individually and collectively

From codependency and unhealthy relationships.

Let us be free individually and collectively

From chemical dependence and all addictive behaviors.

Let us be free from the erroneous idea that we do not need others.

Let us be interdependent knowing who we are and what we bring to the table.

Let us be interdependent realizing the benefits and blessings of others have come to share with us.

It is so, so it is, and we let it be.

Amen and Amen.

Read: I Corinthians 12:12-28

A VETERANS' DAY PRAYER

We bless and celebrate all those who have served in all branches of the services.

Our hearts are full of gratitude for the sacrifices that they have made and continue to make for our safety.

In the spirit of service,

Let us give our time,

In the spirit of service,

Let us give our gifts and talents.

In the spirit of service

Let us give our abilities and sensitivities,

In the spirit of service

Let us give our money.

May all that we say and do be given from the energy of love

It is so, so it is, and so we let it be.

Amen and Amen

Read: Romans 13:1-7

A HALLOWEEN PRAYER

As we celebrate Halloween with our children.

The fun and festivities of the fall,

And get in touch with our own inner child,

Let us remember the truth.

There is only One Power, God.

Therefore, we release any worry and anxiety.

Let us remember the truth.

There is only One Presence, Good.

Therefore, we have no fear of darkness and evil.

Let us remember the truth.

There is only One Energy in the Universe, Love.

Therefore, we are safe and protected.

It is so, so it is, and we so let it be.

Read: Psalm 27

ALL SOULS PRAYER

Take a deep breath.

Feel the life energy that is in each of us.

Take another deep, conscious, and cleansing breath.

Let us take a moment to remember the souls of all of our loved ones who have transitioned.

And breathe

Let us remember the truth that there is no death in reality,

Only higher and higher forms of life.

And breathe

Let us remember the legacy that they left us.

And breathe.

Let us remember the love that they gave us.

And breathe.

Let us remember the lessons that they taught us.

It is so, so it is, and so we let it be.

Amen. Amen.

Read: Ezekiel 18:1-4

A THANKSGIVING PRAYER

Who I AM God made me,

Thank you, God, for making me who I AM.

Where I AM God brought me,

Thank you, God, for bringing me this far.

What I have God gave me,

Thank you, God, for everything you have given me.

What I know God taught me.

Thank you, God, for everything that you have taught me.

Amen.

Read: Psalm 107

A CHRISTMAS PRAYER

May there always be room in your heart for divinity to find a birthing place.

May you be holy as the angels were,

Faithful as the shepherds were,

Humble as the cattle were,

And wise as the men were who brought gifts to Jesus.

May you have the compassion Mary had

The understanding Joseph had,

The support that Elizabeth had

The enthusiasm that Simeon had,

The dedication that Anna had,

May the blessing of the holy child be yours,

not because of his birth long ago,

but because his love is born in you today!

Amen.

Read: Luke 2:21-40

WINTER CELEBRATIONS

We join the consciousness of celebration.

We celebrate anything that brings joy to your heart this season.

Merry Christmas.

Happy Hanukkah.

Happy Kwanza.

Happy Winter Solstice.

Anything that you are celebrating, we are celebrating with you.

We pray that this joy will continue throughout all the seasons of your life.

It is so, so it is, and so we let it be.

Amen.

Read: Romans 12:14-21

THE BIRTHDAY PRAYER

Thank you, God, for another year of life.

Every day and in every way,

I AM getting better and better.

Every week with every peak and valley,

I AM becoming more of who you created me to be.

Every month I learn a bunch of lessons so that I can be all that I AM in you.

Every year may I let go of fear

And become more perfected in love.

This is my day to be courageous.

This is my season to be prosperous.

This is my time to be successful.

It is so, so it is, and so I let it be.

Read: Joshua 1:1-9

THE LABOR AND DELIVERY PRAYER

Our hearts are full of gratitude that we have been chosen to be the parents of this baby.

May the birthing process flow in divine order.

Thank you for every contraction and dilation.

We are grateful for a smooth and safe delivery.

We bless the doctors, nurses, and technicians who are supportive in this process.

We know that this child is coming to earth for a purpose that must be fulfilled.

We appreciate this opportunity to share ourselves with this new life.

It is so, so it is, and so we let it be.

Amen. Amen.

Read: Jeremiah 1:4-10

THE NEW HOME PRAYER

I AM grateful for this new home.

I appreciate this new beginning.

I thank you, God, for this new opportunity.

We bless this space with love and welcome all who enter.

We sanctify this place with joy and see celebrations happening here.

We dedicate this dwelling with peace and are reenergized in this environment.

We know that your divine provision is ensuring that all household expenses are met with ease and breeze of the Holy Spirit.

We know that your divine protection is present all the days that we live here.

It is so, so it is, and so we let it be.

Amen. Amen.

Read Joshua 24:14-27

THE TRANSITION PRAYER: RELEASING A LOVED ONE

_____ has transitioned from this dimension of life (abundant life) to the next dimension of life (eternal life).

I know the truth that _____ did not pass away because _____ memory will never pass away from our hearts.

I know the truth that _____ did not die because there is no death in reality only higher forms of life.

"If this earthly house of this tabernacle be dissolved, we have another building not made by hands (2 Corinthians 5:1).

I know the truth that we did not lose _____ because we know where _____ is.

"To be absent from the body is to be present with the Lord (2 Corinthians 5:8)."

We give ourselves permission to feel mixed emotions about _____'s transition.

We experience sorrow because we will no longer experience _____ in a physical way.

We experience joy because ____ _____ has transitioned to _____ highest good.

Now we finish any unfinished business that we have with _____.

Now we forgive ourselves for anything that was left unsaid, and we say it now in our minds.

Now we forgive ourselves for anything that was left undone, and we do it now in our minds.

Now we forgive _____ for anything that was said or done that was not the highest and the best.

We release _____ and allow _____ to transition to _____ next dimension of life.

Read John 11:1-44

THE WEDDING PRAYER

I bless this couple and their marriage.

Whatever their hands touch is blessed.

Wherever their feet walk is blessed.

They are blessed whenever they come into a place.

They are blessed whenever they leave a place.

They are the head in any situation.

They are never the tail in any experience.

They are above only and not beneath.

They are lenders and not borrowers.

The blessings of God are on their lives.

They are overtaken with good things and good news.

Read: Deuteronomy 28:1-14

Conclusion

Notice that each chapter in this book is called a Prayer Book. Prayer Book I is Daily Life-changing Prayers. Prayer Book II is Life-changing Prayers for Specific Manifestations. Prayer Book III is Personal Life-changing Prayers. Prayer Book IV Life-changing Prayers for Groups. Prayer Book V is Life-changing Prayers for Holidays and Special Occasions.

People of old have said, "your mouth is not a prayer book." This was an indication that anyone can lie, speak profanity or vulgarity. My intention through this book is for your mouth to become a prayer book. As you work with these Life-changing Prayers, I see your mind and your mouth being transformed and I envision your life being a prayer to God.

Made in the USA
Monee, IL
15 October 2023

44506424R00057